Permission **GRANTED**

Advance Praise

"Marcia Coné's *Permission Granted* taps the power of questions and introspection and uses them as springboards to careers and lives of fulfillment."

— **Susan Colantuono**, CEO of Leading Women

"*Permission Granted* is the antidote to limiting thoughts, the action plan for getting unstuck, and the motivational kick to get where you want to go in your life. A must read for women of all ages and life stages."

— **Leah DeCesare**, Author of *Forks, Knives, and Spoons:*
A Novel and the *Naked Parenting* series

"In *Permission Granted*, Marcia Coné has given us an accessible, down to earth guide for women who want to transform their lives. The pages are filled with sophisticated insight that will help women imagine a different reality for themselves. This is coupled with practical advice, a toolkit, really, to help women locate their inner confidence and realize their capacity to transform their own lives. Drawing on her own vast and impressive background as a change maker, Marcia Coné speaks from having been in the trenches of leadership herself and has a genuine mission to help other women face their fears, trust themselves, find confidence, and reach their full potential. The book is a roadmap for women of all ages to getting what they really want in their career and in life."

> — **Dr. Kim Miller, PhD**, Professor and Coordinator
> of Women's and Gender Studies,
> Wheaton College (Norton, MA)

"Permission Granted offers advice, inspiration and tactical tools for moving ahead in a positive direction for your career and your life. Not only that, the book gives the reader a firm reminder that she can have it all - whatever that means to her - and we all can use that reminder!"

> — **Tuti Scott**, Founder and President,
> Imagine Philanthropy

Permission GRANTED

Changing the Paradigm for Women in Leadership

MARCIA A. CONÉ, PhD

NEW YORK

NASHVILLE • MELBOURNE • VANCOUVER

Permission GRANTED
Changing the Paradigm for Women in Leadership

Published in New York, New York, by Morgan James Publishing.
www.MorganJamesPublishing.com

The Morgan James Speakers Group can bring authors to your live event. For more information or to book an event visit The Morgan James Speakers Group at www.TheMorganJamesSpeakersGroup.com.

ISBN 978-1-68350-333-0 paperback
ISBN 978-1-68350-334-7 eBook
Library of Congress Control Number:
2016918418

Cover Design by:
Chris Treccani
www.3dogdesign.net
Interior Design by:
Bonnie Bushman
The Whole Caboodle Graphic Design
Editing:
Grace Kerina
Author's photo courtesy of:
Nuria Chantre

In an effort to support local communities, raise awareness and funds, Morgan James Publishing donates a percentage of all book sales for the life of each book to Habitat for Humanity Peninsula and Greater Williamsburg.

Get involved today! Visit
www.MorganJamesBuilds.com

Dedication

For my daughters, Hannah and Sophia.

Table of Contents

Introduction

"When the student is ready, the teacher will appear."
—Buddha

Have you ever had the experience of finding just the right thing, just when you needed it? Sometimes the right thing comes to you before you even know you need it. The right thing can be a person, course, book, speaker, or one of countless other experiences. The challenge is to be open to the gift when it presents itself.

So often, I've found myself floundering, feeling frustrated, or complaining when the answer was nearby or right in front of my face. I just wasn't open to seeing, hearing, or believing, or wasn't ready to take the first step forward. From my own personal experiences, I know that when we are ready to implement change we become open to and begin searching for a catalyst to help us take those first steps, and then the next steps that naturally and logically follow. Before we know it, we are on the very path we once held ourselves back from stepping onto.

I know, I know – really, I do know – that moving from "I'm stuck. I'm frustrated. I'm not ready. I'm afraid. I can't do this. I shouldn't do this" to being open to change doesn't happen by simply waving a wand or making a wish. It does, however, begin with being willing to entertain the idea of taking that first step into curiosity – into the what-if and how-can-I space. Entertaining possibility, that flicker of feeling that rises within you, is the key to being open to positive change.

So many times, the decision I knew needed to be made was one I sat on for too long, until I'd made the transition harder than it needed to be. For example, knowing it was time to leave an organization or position, or that it was time to lay my cards on the table with myself and jump into the next phase of what needed to be done at the organization, but instead of doing it hedging about whether I was ready or not.

This game of hide and seek is one I seem to recall following me since childhood. Would I risk trying out for the lead in the play? Would I risk auditioning for glee club? What would happen if I left my job? How would I make ends meet? What would people, think, say, believe about me? What if I failed? But, even more so, what if I succeeded? What then? Eventually, I would get to the place where what I thought and, just as important, what I needed, became the most crucial factors in making my way toward what I really wanted. I learned to put one foot in front of the other and edge my way forward.

The process of making a decision to change is one that can take months, years, lifetime – if we let the process run on without intervention. Without fail, every decision I held out on making for longer than I should have, and then made, resulted in my realization that I wished I had moved in that direction much sooner. In fact, I can say the only regrets I have are about decisions that I wish I had made sooner. My thoughts and fears about what lay on the other side of those decisions were usually only that – thoughts and fears. I handed over the responsibility for my happiness, and for what I really wanted in life, to the thought gremlins.

Is It Time for Change?

Change and growth are innate and a necessary part of the human experience. Like the genetic wiring of a seed tells that tells it when it is time to grow; human beings have wiring that tells us when it is time to grow. Like with physical and reproductive maturation process, our bodies move forward because our genetic wiring tells us it is time and, whether we are ready or not, growth happens.

On social, emotional, personal, and professional levels, we have that same genetic wiring that tells us it is time for growth. The difference is that the human mind interferes with that process, allowing us to consider whether we are ready for growth. Albert Einstein is attributed with saying, "The intuitive mind is a sacred gift and the rational mind is a faithful servant. We have created a society that honors the servant and has forgotten the sacred gift."

Our internal wiring, often called *intuition*, gives us notice that it is time for movement leading to growth. We humans can develop a dangerous habit of repeatedly ignoring our gut instinct, believing our rational mind serves our best interests when, in fact, the rational mind can talk us into or out of almost anything. So, rather than paying attention to the nudge, we pay homage to the rational mind that whispers, "I'm not ready. It's too risky. No one has ever done this, or anyone who has done this has not succeeded, so I won't either. Unhappiness is the price I'd pay for the choice I'd make. Taking a risk is too dangerous. Staying safe and in my comfort zone is preferable and best," and on and on. We bury the sacred gift of our intuition until we've shut it down, and we do so to our detriment.

Over time, our choice to not change results in many physical, emotional, and spiritual challenges that are actually symptoms, not root cause. Western medicine and culture try to disconnect the association between intuition and following its advice, thus challenging the cause of the symptoms we experience at work and home. When we don't address the root cause, our symptoms increase, pushing us to pay attention. Roots take hold, go deep, and, before we know it, we've got a whole pattern of behavior that, even if we address the symptoms, remains firmly entrenched.

Isn't This Just Failure Dressed Up?

I grew up in at a time when children were told to be grateful for what they had and not to overextend their reach. "It's best not to want too much and risk failure rather taking on the risks of pursuing your passion." A long, steady, stable job was more important than feeling passionate about your job. If you got it right when you were just out of high school, or even right after college graduation, you were one of the lucky ones. For the rest of us, who may not have gotten it right – well, once you retire you can pursue whatever you like. That was a time when doing the right thing included staying in a marriage even when love, respect, partnership, and kindness was not present. And staying in a bad job was better than not having job, because we couldn't see or believe that there were many other jobs to choose from. It was a time when advice such as "You made your own bed, now lie in it" prevailed. That kind of thinking has permeated generations of us who think that good enough is good enough.

Many of us still believe that making a choice, whether it turns out well or not, is permanent, and so suffering through is preferable to making changes. Because, goodness knows, we shouldn't admit that sometimes our choices are good for a time but eventually may no longer serve us. We may subscribe to the notion that there is no choice-expiration date.

These stances have infiltrated the psyches of many people who feel as though they chose their circumstances and cannot choose otherwise now. We have come to believe that, somehow, the choice to shift our circumstances or position is not honorable, is not a sign of strength, but of weakness, and is a symbol of failure.

Who we are in our personal lives often does not veer too far from who we are as our professional personas. Those who are capable of being two different people, one at home and another at the office, are great at compartmentalizing. Compartmentalizing is a coping strategy to deal with the different and conflicting roles, responsibilities, values, and experiences. This defense mechanism can be an effective short-term tool, but over long periods of time, compartmentalizing can become exhausting, debilitating, and detrimental. Cognitive dissonance occurs when we deny who we are in order to fit our own or other peoples' expectations of who we are "supposed to be." That is a mental game of Ping-Pong that can leave us unable to move forward.

Perhaps you identify with one, some, or all of these cultural, social, and emotional trappings that can keep us from moving forward. If so, the pages that follow are full of ideas, strategies, and tactics for helping you move into a space of openness, opportunity, choice, wholeness, and alignment, by making changes that support your growth. Your natural inclinations and your innate genetic wiring makes you lean toward the sun of what you yearn for, wanting the nourishing light that opens possibility and promise.

We can grow and flower when we reconnect with our intuition, follow our instincts, and trust the process that affirms that we are living beings who have the capacity to adapt to changing environments, landscapes, circumstances, and situations. We can be grounded, healthy, strong, and able to sustain ourselves even as we change.

Together, in this book, we will explore how you can open yourself up to your potential and take steps that will advance your career.

Your potential for growth is worth your time and attention.

How Did I Get Here?

"Thankfully, dreams can change. If we'd all stuck with our first dream, the world would be overrun with cowboys and princesses"
—**Stephen Colbert**

hear this over and over again from clients, students, friends, family: "How did I get here? How did this happen? How did I not see this coming?" Often, when we peel back the layers of how, the information was there all along, but we chose to ignore it.

We ignore the information we need for making decisions that are right for us for a host of reasons. "I don't have time to deal with it now. I don't like the information that's coming in. If I ignore it, it will go away. If I work hard enough it will get better." And more. Our wonderful coping mechanisms serve us in many ways – until we don't notice that they no longer serve us and they become dysfunctional patterns of avoidance that leave us asking how we arrived at this place we don't want to be.

How Much Effort Is Involved?

Have you ever gone out with a group of friends and ordered what everyone else was having? Or couldn't decide where you wanted to eat so ended up at the same place you always go, eating the same thing you always order? There is nothing inherently wrong with having the same dinner at the same place over and over again, or doing the same thing over and over again, except when we do so because making a decision to do something different feels like it takes too much effort, or when we give in to the belief that we'll eventually have a different experience that will lead to different outcomes. A certain amount of ritual and routine is human and helps with productivity, consistency, and efficiency, and there is a place for that. However, it becomes a troubling problem when you do the same things, even though you are seeking different results.

We often conduct our interactions at home and at work to essentially replicate the same conversational patterns. Our hope is that the receiver will suddenly understand or hear us differently. Or that somehow, a small tweak in our tone or seriousness will evoke the sense that we really mean it this time. When we don't get the result we want, we tell ourselves we tried, we put ourselves out there, but really we set up the same situation and expected it to go differently. If we are honest, we find some level of comfort in putting the responsibility for the sameness of our lives on our boss, our colleagues, our spouse, our children.

A friend of mine always says, "Nothing changes if nothing really changes." Have you ever noticed that you come home after a shopping trip with essentially the same blouse, skirt, suit, tie you already have a closet full of? We go out looking for something new and come home with our good old standbys.

When we are not intentional about what we want, and when we don't act differently, it should come as no surprise when we keep serving up the same thing. Real change, lasting change, is going to take some effort.

At work, when we make decisions not to contribute to the conversation, to opt out of new experiences or opportunities, to not challenge ourselves or others, we are being quite selfish. Yes, I'm saying that holding back is driven by selfishness, because we are trying to avoid the discomfort or fear or pain that might come with being more true and honest.

Here's where I am going with all of this: *What if liberating yourself is the very thing that will liberate others?*

We dress up our motivation and call it *selflessness,* when really it's *self-abdication.* We make others responsible for our frustrations and decisions, for our likes, dislikes, lack of promotions, and careers rather than being truthful with ourselves and others about what we want, who we really are, and what is holding us back.

Do We Fit In?

Substantial psychological research has empirically demonstrated that a status quo bias is commonplace among humans. We want to fit in, because we consider it safe. Many of us work very hard at staying in our comfort zone and riding the status quo. We are wired to be biased toward the status quo, to keep things pretty much as they are and avoid change. This becomes irrational when there is no evidence that supports keeping things the same. When we are not producing our desired outcome by continuing to do the same thing – that's when we need to risk a change.

Often, we don't even recognize that there are other ways of doing things, because the status quo is all we've ever noticed. As humans, and certainly as evidenced by our culture, we are pushed, cajoled, shamed, and humiliated into assimilation. We may want very badly to fit in – even when fitting in means aligning with the counter culture. The human brain is evolutionarily wired to resist behavior that risks alienation because breaking away from the tribe used to mean danger and death. So we quickly and unthinkingly submit to what is standard, common, or accepted – instead of considering how doing so may have fatal consequences.

And so it is with our careers.

Businesses and organizations all have a cultures of their own – both formal and informal. Employees quickly learn the ropes about how, when, and where to line up. We are indoctrinated about how things are done and advised to see how the chain of command really works. Even if you've been hired to be the disruptor or the innovator, the push to assimilate and to align with company culture and norms is enormous. More often than not, the new employee who's brought in to be a disruptor starts to look, sound, and work according to the rules. They do so in order to survive. It's human nature to do all we can to survive.

But it's also human nature to grow.

Where's the Proof?

We get stuck in perpetuating assumptions, myths, fear, and resistance to change, *even when they don't serve us or our cause*. We make assumptions every day and test them out routinely. We assume that 30 minutes is enough time to get from our home to the office, that meetings will finish on time, and so on. In general, we are okay with making these assumptions and updating them to avoid miscalculating time or resources if something has changed.

When we try to revise our assumptions about our careers, however, we can trigger some hefty emotions that trip us up. Suddenly, our ability to take risks and to revise our calculations regarding time, and resources related to the risk paralyzes us. We evaluate what we will and won't do at work based heavily on our assumptions.

Harvard researchers Robert Kegan and Lisa Lahey developed a coaching process called Immunity to Change. What was pivotal for me about learning their process was realizing the opportunity it gives us to face up to our assumptions and take on the task of challenging them. Identifying an assumption helps us see the barriers we have constructed and test the assumption, and that may inform and change beliefs we've held that are holding us back. Challenging our assumptions is a way of reframing that can powerfully shift thinking and free us to move forward.

As Kegan and Lahey also point out, it's our hidden assumptions about competing commitments that keep us from achieving what we want. We may set goals or entertain dreams for our careers without really considering the intended and unintended outcomes. Other times, we may be so buried in overthinking that we forfeit the intended and unintended outcomes without ever taking a shot at it.

Similarly, adopting myths as truths can wedge its way into our thinking. Accounts and tales of what happened to other employees, about who is eligible for a promotion, about speaking up, offering ideas, having opinions, about working hard and keeping your nose to the grindstone, about getting noticed – such myths are part of what helps keep us stuck in an idling state. Many of us spend so much time working hard and get frustrated when we realize our hard work isn't paying off. Usually, at that point, we push ourselves to work even harder, assuming that, somehow, more of the same hard work will make a difference.

And so the cycle continues.

We perpetuate the myth of hard work and psychologically punish ourselves over and over. Hard work for the sake of hard work is a self-punishment. When we are in that space we cannot see that we are limiting ourselves. We are saying that there is something wrong with us and/or our work ethic, rather than evaluating the situation more closely to see what is really happening.

I'm not advocating that we not give our best work. Quite the opposite. Our best work doesn't come when we are forcing ourselves to try to make things happen through hard work when working harder cannot achieve our goal. No amount of air can fill a punctured tire. The tire requires a patch or replacing. Your repeated efforts to fill the punctured tire – your hard work toward a direction you may not want to actually go – has no bearing on the reality of the situation. In fact, your focus on the "hard work" has kept you from seeing the bigger picture and finding solutions.

How Do We Respond?

Playing it safe with your career and in your current position can also be a major factor in getting you to a point of feeling stuck, dissatisfied, or unclear about what you really want. Playing it safe means that fear directs your actions or inaction. Playing it safe at work can look like this: not networking with colleagues or others in your industry and beyond; not scheduling one-on-one meetings with your boss and other leaders in the company; not asking for feedback; doing it yourself because you don't trust your team; not asking for opportunities or assignments that stretch you.

When we are about to do something outside of our comfort zone or normal way of being, our bodies signal to us through a physiological reaction informing us there is some threat. If you take a moment and think about a specific time when you were about to do something new, you can likely conjure up the feelings of discomfort and where they lived in your body.

That's the physiological response. What's crucial is what happens *after* that response. Often this physiological response is all we pay attention to, so we decide that the perceived threat is real and we stop before we even get started. The flight-or-fight response is very real and provides important information for us to consider. In many cases, the response doesn't signal a red light, but rather a yellow light telling you to proceed with caution. Yet many of us misinterpret the physiological information over and over again without ever questioning our response or getting curious about what the information is telling us.

We have the opportunity to challenge ourselves and process the physiological information we are receiving by asking a few simple questions:

- "What other information do I need?"
- "Is what I perceive actually true?"
- "What assumptions have I made?"
- "What myths am I preserving?"

- "What small steps can I take to test out what I'm experiencing?"
- "How can I move forward?"

Even when we have answered all of these questions and determined that we are safe to take a risk, we can still be resistant to change. Volumes of research from the fields of psychology, health care, social work, and other disciplines tell us that humans are resistant to change even when the change is in their best interest. Don't believe me? Do you know anyone who was told they must make a change or put their health and their life at risk? How hard was it for them to make those changes, even knowing what was at stake?

How do you know if this is you? Resistance to change takes many forms, with avoidance, sabotage, aggressiveness, and passivity being some of the most common. You may have a low tolerance for change. You may mistrust in general and have reason to mistrust the circumstances or the individuals involved in a situation. Over time, our reaction and resistance to change can form patterns and ways of being that end up getting in our way.

When we feel stuck and resistant to change, it's often because we also feel a loss of control. An unintended consequence of resisting change because you feel a loss of control is that the loss results anyway. The very thing you fear – loss of control – is what you end up having because you resist change. As a result, you lose control of the situation and your ability to move through the change in ways that support you.

Resistance to change can also manifest itself in highly successful people. We can engage in a business practice or process that works, and works well. So we ask ourselves, why change it if it works? Success is often not seen as an indicator of a need to make change. Yet, so many successful leaders I've had the honor to talk with over the years have shared stories of how they knew it was time to make a change – for themselves and/or for the business – even though things were going well.

When something works, we take for granted how and why it works and may overlook whether it could work better. In this way, success can be a blind spot that leads to trouble down the road. You can rest on your laurels, but if you do, you can also rest assured that there is someone coming on your heels whose curiosity will lead to a new innovation.

At more than one point in my own career, I've found myself feeling stuck and frustrated. I thought it to be such an odd experience, given how well things were going. Upon closer examination, I realized that each time I felt stuck it was a message to me that it was time to grow; to invite change. That feeling of being stuck represented a pivotal moment when I had a decision to make. Stay where it was good enough? Or move forward? Those moments of clarity often came with the realization that my own experience as a leader was mirrored in the organization and it was time for the organization to grow, too.

A wise and caring individual who was mentoring me early in my career gave me this piece of advice: You cannot take anyone somewhere you are not willing to go yourself. How we lead and serve others is informed and directed by how we lead and support ourselves.

Essentially, whether we are talking about believing our assumptions, promulgating myths, or inciting fear, it's about the resistance to change.

What's the solution? Reframing the situation. When we reframe, we are able to stand back and change our point of reference to a new perspective.

What's in Your Viewfinder?

Do our assumptions, beliefs, and actions hold true when we look at the situation from another viewpoint? Reframing allows us to consider the circumstance or situation through a new lens or set of lenses. An intended result is that we also change our emotional state related to the situation. Repeatedly, we assign meanings to events, activities, situations, circumstances that are based on how we interpret those events. If we feel happy when something occurs, we assign the inherent meaning of happiness. Our underlying motivation has to do with the beliefs and assumptions we hold about an event. The challenge is to find our positive intent behind all of those assigned meanings and bring them to the surface to be examined in the light of truth. Sometimes it's necessary to take a few steps back to look from another perspective.

Your thoughts matter. They frame how you deliberate, act, and feel. If your thoughts are negative and left unchecked, then the lens through which you view your circumstances will be negative.

How you talk to yourself matters. Our self-talk informs our moods, our associations with events and individuals, and becomes a self-fulfilling prophesy. My uncle Al was known for saying, "Can't never could," and he's right. If you think you can't, well, you can't. I'd also add to his saying that "Won't never will." It is only when we entertain the idea that we *can* and that we *will* achieve, advance, or start whatever we are thinking about doing and want to do that it actually becomes possible.

When I was thirteen years old, the public library in my hometown was one of my favorite places. It still is. Back then, the books, the quietness, and the possibility of interacting with my grandmother, who was one of the librarians, made it a special place. Always on the look-out for a good book, I stumbled on Norman Vincent Peale's *The Power of Positive Thinking* and decided to read it. Serendipity shined upon me that day. I devoured the book and then read it again. The book's lessons remain with me to this day. Realizing, at that young age, that my thoughts could inform and transform any circumstance or situation seemed like a rite of passage like no other.

But there are plenty of times that I've lost sight of or forgotten about that insight. Eventually, I do find my way back to my senses enough to ask myself: "What are my thoughts?" and "How am I framing the situation?" and "What thoughts and framing will help me in the moment?" Without fail, the moment I change my emotional state, my relationship with the situation changes and the path unfolds.

Often, the way we get here, to finding ourselves feeling stuck, derailed, or hindered, resides in our thoughts and, as a natural and logical consequence, how we experience what is happening. Shifting our thoughts shifts our perceptions and opens up conduits for change. Our ability to see things differently allows different choices, opportunities, and solutions to emerge. No longer stuck, we see that there are a myriad of responses or actions that can be taken.

The choice, as always, is ours. Are we ready to accept that where we are, in large part, is exactly where we directed ourselves to be *and* that we can redirect ourselves? We can challenge our assumptions, stop believing the myths, tackle fear, and bust through our resistance to change by shifting the way we think and by coaching ourselves to reframe the situation and embrace new perspectives.

The choice to redirect ourselves requires one small step: being open to changing our thoughts.

What Keeps Me Here
Where I Don't Want to Be?

"If you don't risk anything, you risk even more"
—Erica Jong

I f we are honest with ourselves, we are likely to be able to identify some of the decisions, or lack thereof, that got us to here, where we don't want to be. At the time we made the decisions (or avoided making them – which is really making a decision) that got us here, we were doing the best we could do at the time. I truly believe that we all do the best we can in each moment.

There are times when we decide very consciously that what we are about to do is the best effort we can muster. We ascertain that we have a finite amount of energy and, based on that, we do what we can, knowing it isn't necessarily going to get us to where we want to be.

When we consciously or unconsciously make decisions that have us opting out of acting in our own best interests, we create patterns of behavior that we eventually earnestly justify and defend.

It is that pattern of collective not-quite-true decisions, actions, and inactions that got us *here*, and that keeps us where we don't want to be.

We, as human beings, are capable of self-reflection. We can look back and figure out how we might have handled moments differently. I know from the experiences of my clients, as well as my own personal experiences, that critical, defining moments present themselves regularly. When they do, we have the choice of repeating the same patterns – the pattern that got us here where we don't really want to be – or taking a path we have not yet taken.

Stepping out of habits and into new behaviors can be daunting. Many choose to ignore trying another way of responding to the opportunity, and stay the course, denying the need for change. Denial is a powerful defense mechanism that keeps us where we are. Sometimes, without fully realizing it, we justify our decisions, behaviors, and responses because they allow us to remain the same.

Maybe we convince ourselves that we *have* taken a different tack, because the circumstances or players are different this time and so, we reason, the choice we are making is, therefore, different. But that is not really taking a different path – one with a good chance of getting us to a different place.

The mental reasoning that allowed us to get here was made of irrational thinking. We tend to rely on habits and underestimate our ability to *think* our way into or out of a multitude of circumstances and situations on a daily basis. So, what would happen if, when opportunity presented itself, we were to consciously think about what to do before we made a decision and took action?

Move Forward or Get Lost in Mind Clutter?

When an opportunity presents itself, mustering enough courage to take those first steps in a new direction can feel both amazing and tenuous. We may get excited about the possibilities ahead of us and map out a plan of action, or we may get lost in the clutter that fills our thoughts. Unfortunately, when it's time to take action, we may begin to think about the opportunity and ourselves in relation to the opportunity in disparaging ways. This *habit* is neither helpful nor truthful and leads us to make decisions that are based on *feelings* rather than *facts*. It is often at this very early point that we turn back and do the same things again that we've always done.

Think about this for a few minutes. How do we speak to ourselves when we are out of our comfort zone? If we spoke to those we love the same way we speak to ourselves, we'd end up alone and unhappy, and yet we seem to think it's okay to subject ourselves to that kind of negativity and scrutiny.

It's so easy to get caught up in mind clutter. It starts with "What am I doing? How could I have thought this was a good idea? I don't have the qualifications! I've never done this before. The financial, emotional, and physical costs are too high." We start to doubt ourselves and fill our minds with junk.

Then we start in on self-talk that is full of shame about being the source of the problem. "How could I have been so stupid? Why didn't I see this before? If only I had..." and on it goes, until the heaviness of how we feel becomes too much to bear. That's when letting go of the opportunity seems to be the right thing to do to stop the pain.

It's usually at this point that we pop in to a colleague's office to "process." They play their role perfectly and we leave feeling vindicated... and there the processing ends. Some of us will then seek out others who will support the conclusion we and our colleague just arrived at, and that provides us with further evidence to support our decision to play it safe.

We've kept the focus on ourselves. As a result, we don't see the bigger picture. We don't see how much limiting ourselves limits others. We reason that what we're doing is best for others, the company, our family. We lay the responsibility at the feet of others rather than owning up to what's really going on. Here again, we play at selflessness when really we've indulged in a moment of abandoning ourselves, abdicating our primary role of being responsible for ourselves.

What's really going on here is that an opportunity for growth presented itself, we saw the opportunity, felt uncomfortable, and decided to turn back and go down our usual path of doing things and of processing. We took the same path that got us, and keeps us, here – where we say we don't want to be.

Is "Good Enough" Good Enough?

At one time or another, the tendency to do nothing – even though circumstances or situations have made it clear that action is required of us – is obvious to us, but we cannot seem to muster the courage to step forward. We coach ourselves in ways that support our delay: "It's best to wait and see how things develop." We play the game of wait-and-see, telling ourselves that when we have more information we'll address the situation. We know how to delay for as long as possible, with the hope that things will change enough to make taking action no longer necessary, or with the hope that someone else will step forward and take responsibility. Years later, we find we are still in the very same place.

Often the additional information we waited for only confirmed what we already knew. The passage of time did not provide space for us to grow out of or into the next level. Things didn't just "work themselves out." Ten years later here we are – still frustrated, still unhappy, still waiting for the right manager or director who will value our contributions. Waiting, waiting for something to happen to us or for us.

Inertia, by definition, requires external force to overcome. But human inertia can often withstand a great deal of external force and still leave us unchanged. In the moment, the external force may temporarily move us off our center, but eventually we creep back to that habitual center. Or we use external rewards as motivators, rather than setting our sights on a direction that's internally motivated, and find that the new title, new company, or increase in salary just isn't worth it. Health, financial, relationship, political, legal, and other crises come at us, telling us it is time to do something different, but we cannot bring ourselves to change. We tell ourselves those external forces are bad luck or situational or signs telling us to stay where we are, rather than seeing them as indicators pointing us in the direction of change.

Who Can We Trust, If Not Ourselves, First?

A few years ago, I met with a colleague who, over the past two decades, had become a reliable and truth-telling sounding board for me. While sharing all of the things that were going on in the organization I worked for at the time, I also shared my growing frustration about being unable to get to new ideas and opportunities or to what I wanted and needed for my personal well-being and professional growth. I explained that, by the time I attended to all of my various responsibilities and commitments, there wasn't any time to left for other pursuits.

My friend turned to me and flatly said, "What about your commitments to yourself? What happens to you when you don't follow through on your commitments to you?"

I was startled, because I had never considered that I wasn't keeping commitments to myself. I had no response. Taking opportunity of my silence, my friend went on to share with me something she had learned about herself a few years before. She, like me, was committed to her work and to the business she worked for. Over and over, she would "adjust" her schedule so that she could attend meetings that had been arranged at the last minute. She also found herself working on weekends to complete projects, often as a result of others not keeping to their timelines. She told me that every time she said yes, she was breaking her commitments to herself – because these intrusions into her schedule meant that her commitment to self-care (like getting to her yoga class, being present for and spending time with her family on the weekends) weren't being kept, and that included time she had scheduled for new projects, writing, reading, and engaging with colleagues in her sector.

In my mind, as she talked, I kept thinking, "Yes, but being flexible is what we have to do. It's what is required. So I miss out on a few things at home or a few yoga classes – that's the price of working, and it's what leads to success."

As if she was reading my mind, my friend explained how she came to realize that she wasn't prioritizing her own commitments at work or at home. She became the person everyone relied on to help them get *their* work done or to manage the latest crisis. They did so because they knew they could, and doing so freed them up to keep their own commitments.

Not keeping commitments to ourselves is deeply problematic, whether we are talking about professional or personal commitments. When we break commitments to ourselves, we let ourselves down. We train ourselves to understand that we will not be there for ourselves. We assume that allowing the priorities of others to supersede our own means we are doing "the right thing." For many of us, this pattern continues until the priorities of others completely overtake our own, at which point we can become bitter and resentful without really knowing why.

I know plenty of dyed-in-the-wool martyrs who believe that their "kindness" when they prioritize others' needs over their own is other-focused, an act of selflessness. But the reality is that the emotional satisfaction we get from prioritizing everyone else is one of the reasons we keep extending and overextending ourselves. In doing so, we are not valuing ourselves.

This pattern pecks away at our sense of self. On the one hand, we create a sense of satisfaction from helping others, we receive feedback or praise that supports that feeling, *and* we create a situation of not being trustworthy and reliable to ourselves. Typically, we'll need additional external praise to offset the discomfort. Eventually, we relinquish our own self-worth. Our value is based on how others asses our value. When we are dependent on external praise and admiration, we will go to many lengths to keep that praise coming. Even if it means undervaluing our commitments to ourselves.

When we do this in the workplace, we set ourselves up to have less authority and we risk being viewed as incompetent. If we are busy prioritizing everyone else's work, ours must not be as important or as pressing. We aren't allowing ourselves to invest time and energy into creative and innovate ways to advance our projects or products.

Are You Busy or Idle?

Keeping ourselves busy all the time typically has the opposite effect than the one we intend. It keeps us active, but diminishes the effect of our actions. It keeps us from being able to think deeply before we act. Rather than appearing diligent and hardworking, we are often seen as unavailable, otherwise occupied, harried, and tired.

Here's a question for you: How many of your most creative moments happen when you are in the shower? How about while driving, walking the dog, or preparing dinner? For me and many of the folks I have worked with – and I'm guessing for you, too – the answer is that a lot of your creative ideas pop up at odd times when we're relaxed and doing something unrelated to the issue.

I used to wonder why those creative moments popped up at seemingly odd times.

In 2010 I had just completed my PhD and was preparing for my graduation ceremony. During the time I had been studying for my degree, I was also working full-time, running a nonprofit organization, raising two daughters as a single parent, and consulting and teaching across the country. (I know; I know – I was a bit busy.)

One afternoon my cap and gown arrived. I put the package aside, thinking I'd open it later when I "had time." But I kept staring at that package, and the more I looked at it the more I couldn't stop thinking about it. So I opened it up and put on the cap and gown.

As I stood there for quite some time and took in the moment, a feeling washed over me and opened up space for this question: "Why am I always too busy to do these small things?" My answer taught me something very poignant: My busyness was burying me.

We become so frustrated when we get buried in the complexity of managing our lives, and yet sometimes we can experience a shift and see that things are actually very simple. Giving ourselves *white space* – taking time for a break, for moments of rest and reflection – allows us to get clear about what matters.

Offices are often where we go to hide. We sit in our office hour upon hour. We're the first one in and the last one to leave. And we look busy the whole time we are in there. Our message is clear: I'm too busy to engage; too busy to connect; too busy to take a moment to reflect and get clear and be honest about what I'm doing and where I want to go from here.

It's so easy to hide in all the busyness.

It so easy to get buried and hide from our potential.

But it's up to us – not anyone else – to give ourselves permission to step back into that white space and look around. We can choose not to allow ourselves to get buried in the complexity of our lives.

You have to be the one to give that gift to yourself every day.

————

So, what does it look like when we get buried – lose the car keys, get sick, wade through five meetings to make a decision that could have been made in one, take months to hire somebody, feel unable to move forward on the most pressing priorities, can't even find our shoes (have you ever left the house with your slippers on, or wearing two different styles of shoes)?

A few years ago, a client of mine who was grumbling about her senior manager provided a good example of busyness. Here's what she shared: "My senior manager is always buried somewhere in her office. You can't get to her and she isn't coming to us. We need her creativity, insight, and support to get some of our projects off the ground. We need her to lead, not hide out in her office." My client went on to say that she believed her manager didn't trust the team, because she wasn't delegating work and would rather work more hours than hand off a few opportunities the other team members were keen to take on.

Our peers and staff know when we are hiding out *and* they know that keeping busy is a justification for hiding and avoiding. Ultimately, we will pay a hefty price for behaving like this, for hiding out in our busyness.

Busy keeps us from connecting and building relationships.

What's the Difference?

Denial, mental clutter, not keeping our personal commitments, and our attachment to being busy are powerful factors that keep us where we are. These subtle and not so subtle habits are employed by us to keep us from going outside our comfort zone, to keep us from making changes.

Curiosity about our actions and thoughts create inroads to open-mindedness. So question and challenge your thoughts. Ask yourself, "How do I know this to be true?" Look beneath the surface to discover your assumptions. This requires a level of honesty and a commitment to breaking through old patterns and habits. It's striking out in a new direction, and it's going to feel different. Remind yourself that it should.

Let go of the need to be able to control and forecast outcomes. We have plenty of life experience that informs us that the unfolding of activities, events, and relationships is the process of living. We aren't in control of much of anything at the end of the day. We just like to believe we are.

Trust that the path unfolds as it should, and that you will know exactly what you need to know at the right time. Stop perpetuating your own myths that your current situation is safe and secure. We can be in the driver's seat, getting ourselves to the next destination, or we can be a backseat driver waiting to be taken somewhere.

You can rebuild self-trust by creating white space – personal, unscheduled open time in your daily schedule that is just for thinking, reflecting, reading, being – and for calendaring times for the commitments you choose. You can see these white space appointments as being equally as important as your other meetings and deadlines.

Make sure to get out of your office. Leave the phone behind. Connect with yourself and with others.

―――――

If we as leaders value ourselves, take time to make creativity and white space a priority, give ourselves the opportunity to see the world and, thus, see our worries, our responsibilities, our roles a little differently, even for a short time each day, it will change the way we work, think, and lead. In doing this, we also model it for others, so that they can see the positive effects and do the same.

It can be very helpful to find truth-tellers – colleagues who will hold you accountable by being honest and straightforward with you, with kindness and compassion.

Be a truth-teller. Be honest.

Repair your relationship with yourself in order to help others. How? Stop the negative self-talk by checking in with yourself and asking, "Is that thought true?" If not, "What is true?" If it's true, "What will we do to change that?" If you don't want to change that, then accept that as your choice and value that choice. Embrace it and see it as a strength.

Set your priorities and stay accountable to them.

Rebuild trust by doing what's in your best interest. That is usually in everyone's best interest. Remove the badge of "I'm too busy" and engage in opportunities for creativity and innovation.

Applying these mindsets will loosen the frustration that arises when we can't seem to find our way forward. When we engage in self-determination, we proceed because of our choices and we can confidently own that, no longer defending ourselves, because we're actively defining our direction. The feeling of "good enough" will be replaced with appreciation for what led us to where we are now, because we are here intentionally.

When we cultivate lives and careers rooted in intentional thoughts, behaviors, and actions, we embrace self-kindness and compassion. It is in this place and space that we are capable of being truly effective with others, because we meet them from a place of wholeness and sureness.

This is the difference that can make all the difference.

Why Am I So Afraid of Change?

"You must do the things you think you cannot do."
—Eleanor Roosevelt

W e are constantly in a state of change and so is the world around us, yet much of this change happens without our knowing. We accept a certain level of ambiguity and, thus, we also accept a certain level of change as a result. It's the small unnoticeable changes over time that create the big changes. We don't see the big change – meaning the end result – happening or coming and so, when it does, as a result of all the little changes, we are ready for it. Or we've accepted that there was little we could do and it seemed to have little impact on us so we let things move forward with little to no thought or consideration.

When we are directly called or asked to change is when things get complicated.

Are You Misinterpreting Your Warning Light?

Fear is a powerful emotion. Emotion is often what drives the decisions we make about when and whether to change. We give our attention to the thoughts that consume us, even when they are not in the direction of our hopes and dreams. What might we do if we spent as much energy on believing what is possible rather than on our fears? When we turn our attention to our hopes and dreams, we are more apt to notice pieces of information, relationships, and ideas that lead us in the direction of the desired change.

Why did we not see them before? Because we were not open to them and, now, we are. When we direct our thoughts to anxiety, distress, apprehension, and worst-case scenarios, we are just as apt to find plenty of evidence that supports and reinforces that thinking.

When faced with major decisions that required significant change, I have found that *making* the decision is the most difficult part of the process. What I am really doing as I try to make that decision to change is trying to control the change process for myself and for the people involved – right down to how they will feel. Externally controlling things gives us an artificial *sense* of internal control. We aren't actually successful when we use this tactic, because we are essentially enforcing our process on others. While it may feel "easier" or "kinder" in the moment, nothing could be further from the truth, and the costs to us and those around us are substantial.

Think about it. Toddlers don't like to be told what to do and how to do it. They want to explore and figure it out for themselves to understand the way things work. This need to engage and figure things out for ourselves is something that stays with many of us throughout our lives. We come to expect and need these experiences in order to construct meaning and context. And we deserve the right to self-determine.

We are best served by figuring out what has us feeling out of control and dealing with those thoughts and feelings. When we express what is really going on from our perspective, we assume nothing and open up the opportunity to have thoughtful conversations and meaningful interactions. We take responsibility for our thoughts and actions and allow others to do the same.

Do you know anyone who likes to be told to change and, oh, by the way, here's how you'll be making that change? Nope, me either! Yet, we continue to do this because we assume that our colleagues, peers, and family members are incapable of it and/or that we are responsible for making everything okay for everyone.

That fact is, most people are capable. Our challenge is to let go and allow others to self-determine and stay in our own process. At the end of the day, all we are responsible for is ourselves.

When we finally make a decision, what follows is far more easily navigated than we could have imagined or than we wanted to believe.

As long as we believe change is difficult, we have the rationale we are looking for to support not making a decision. When we let go of that fear-based thinking, and the need to control the outcome for those around us, we open ourselves to exploring the natural and logical consequences that follow a choice. And we realize that there are a series of opportunities and choices to make along the way to what we want.

As much as we try, we cannot usually predict the outcome in fine detail. We can, however, make choices in the *direction* of our preferred outcome. Fear is a yellow light – telling us to proceed with caution, but not to stop altogether. That yellow light of fear is not always going to turn into a red light indicating it's time to get out. Physical sensations, thoughts, and emotions help us check in and question whether what we are feeling and experiencing is real or is flights of fantasy-based fear.

We have the power within us to make the experience of change easier by paying attention to our feelings.

Do You Want to Make a Difference?

In 2010 I received a fellowship that allowed me to travel across Scandinavia to experience countries that were ranked in the top five for women's equality. During my first stop, in Iceland, it became increasingly clear to me that the organization I was leading back home was at a crossroads. It could continue as it was or it could take a big risk which, if successful, would significantly advance the mission of the organization.

Why would we hesitate to make choices that would advance the mission of the organization and improve the lives of countless women and girls and their families?

Peel the layers to look well below the surface and there lurked many competing circumstances. The organization was doing very well just as it was. Changing how we did business would mean change for other organizations in the community, which had financial implications for us all. It would mean stepping out into an arena in which the organization was less known. It would mean putting our values and our plans out there for all to judge. And it would require vulnerability – on the part of the organization, the board, and me, as the organization's leader.

When everything looks good and is running smoothly, even when change is in our best interest, there is tremendous pressure, internally and externally, to remain right where we are. The pressure to fit in and not veer too far off cultural norms is significant and, many would say, necessary for survival. Not in terms of actual life or death, but in terms of professional and social standing, veering away from the status quo can mean the difference between fitting in and getting along or going it alone – and, thereby, making a real difference.

If we are interested in making a difference, then we must be willing to move away from conventional wisdom and thinking and tolerate not fitting in.

While in Finland, I experienced the outdoor markets in the capital city of Helsinki. My hotel room was right on the marina and the marketplace was set up along the docks. Huge orange tents were set up and vendors, lined up in every space available, sold everything from furs and knives to fruits and vegetables. Adjacent to those tents was a small set of buildings where the indoor market place was set up for year-round shopping and for stalls selling local foods and wares. In between those two places a small fishing boat was pulled up against the dock – stern side facing the concrete path.

One morning I ventured down to speak to the man who owned this boat. My curiosity was not about what he was selling. – I could see his fish, fruits, and vegetables from my window – but about why he chose not to join those under the orange tents or in the old market hall. His answer was simple and yet profound, "I stay on my boat because it is who I am and the best way for me to stand out from all of the others. We are here doing the same thing, selling our goods, but that doesn't mean we have to set up in exactly the same way." Non-conformity made him productive and viable among the many vendors.

Playing the same "game" that everyone else is playing means you are trying to mimic someone else's way of leading. When we step into who we really are and accept that we can lead and live better from exactly who we are, we find our rhythm. We stand out, not by being exactly like everyone else, but by being exactly who we are and bringing that to the structures that govern how we work, play, or sell.

Freedom comes from being exactly who we are in every circumstance.

Is Your Focus *on* the Business or *in* the Business?

In Sweden, I entered a lovely small shop. The owner of the shop was busy at her sewing machine, working on adding to the line of products she was selling. Her work was amazing, and I asked where else I could find her stores in Sweden and beyond, secretly hoping there was at least one store in New York City. She responded that while she'd hoped to have other shops one day, for now she was too busy doing all of the day-to-day activities regarding design, production, sales, marketing, and administration.

As I left the shop and walked on, a thought entered my mind: The shop owner was heavily focused *in* the business rather than *on* her business. Because she was unwilling to risk hiring the right folks or engaging consultants to help out, it was unlikely that she'd ever get to a place of working on the business to expand its reach. Her dream of owning multiple shops was not likely to become a reality if she continued to do everything all on her own.

Asking for help can be challenging for many of us, but if we want to be our best selves and work at the highest levels we are called to, then we must ask for and accept help. We must keep our focus on the big picture while advancing the day-to day-tasks.

This also means being willing to let go of some of our tasks and allowing them to move into the capable hands of our staff and teams. Our focus should be *on* the business and how to grow and improve what we do every day. Strong leaders and managers focus on the business itself. It's where our creative juices flow and where we can showcase our innovation, strategic thinking, decision-making, and risk-taking. Doing so ensures that the needs of our clients and customers, as well as our staff and investors, remain our top priority.

Let's revisit busyness for a moment here. Often when we are busy we forego what we really want. Being busy keeps us working *in* the business rather than *on* the business. If you are so busy doing your work to get to "almost perfect" and/or micro managing others' work, or doing the work that others might do, you are deep in the weeds of *in* the business. Being in the weeds means you cannot view the whole business and see where things connect or don't in the bigger picture. You can't see the whole view of how the organization's systems are working or malfunctioning, and you can't engage your creativity and innovation to advance the business. Don't get me wrong, all businesses need folks who are good at maintaining and keeping the day-to-day processes happening. But when we are managing and leading others, we must keep our eyes on the bigger picture.

We give others opportunities to grow when we create growth opportunities for ourselves.

Do We Have to Leave Our Comfort Zone?

Many argue for staying in our comfort zone, which feels safe and secure and where we play to our strengths. Usually, our success comes from being very good at what we do. That's what leads us to be promoted. Once promoted, we often fail to see that what got us to the new position or opportunity isn't what will keep us there or what will move us on to the next position or opportunity.

Human nature is complicated. When we experience success we are motivated to take another step in that direction. It's important for us to feel that we can accomplish tasks, meet challenges, and learn new activities, but we often use the same tools, techniques, and thoughts we used for our last success to engage with the next opportunity. And then we experience frustration. What worked for us then isn't working for us now. Although history should inform us, we shouldn't seek to replicate it exactly as is without reflection. Contexts change, the players change, resources become more available or unavailable, what worked in once instance or location doesn't necessarily work in another. Disappointment or weariness can ensure that we find ourselves trying harder to implement or execute what we already know how to implement and execute – even though it's no longer working.

Dissatisfaction with our team or staff can result, because we can't understand why what we know and are good at doing isn't working. It can't be us, so it must be them. Blame, whether openly expressed or secretly held, builds resentment and means you are unwilling to accept responsibility. When we don't own our responsibility for our actions and behavior we become part of the problem rather than part of the solution. We get so worried about covering our own back we forget our job is about covering others' backs.

Here's where trust in relationships breaks down. Communication slows to a halt and everyone takes cover and points fingers. We, as managers and leaders, set the tone for our teams, departments, and businesses. The tone we set is all about communication and relationships – with ourselves and with others. Our relationships with others are reflections of our relationship with ourselves.

When we get comfortable with a certain way of thinking, being, and behaving, we miss important cues that tell us to expand or contract, speed up or slow down, or do something altogether different. Stepping away from a role or responsibility that we are good at to engage in unknown territory can be paralyzing. We know we have to take that step forward, but it feels like a jump between two rocks, with a deep valley below and a huge fall if we don't make it or if our foot slips. From my experience, that is exactly what change feels like. Heart racing, panic flowing, mind calculating how to do it or why not to do it. It is mental, physiological, emotional, and it's all happening at the same time. It can be overwhelming and consuming. We find ourselves saying, "Make this go away" and "I don't have to do this now" and "Why did I think going out this far was a good idea?" and even "Who do I think I am to be taking this on?"

It's in that moment, which is usually only seconds long, that we may opt to stay on our rock and view the valley below, because the leap to the next rock seems far too intimidating. All of the energy that buzzes as adrenaline rises when we are about to do something unknown stops as we move back into our comfort zone. For a while, we can convince ourselves that our decision was the best one and everything will be just fine from here on. We keep up the pretense that we are not stuck in a holding pattern on our safe rock.

Except that, on the other side of that leap, after that step that seems too risky to take, confidence, energy, and passion are waiting for us.

Our comfort zone is often where we are stuck, depressed, frustrated, and disengaged. We make excuses for why we weren't ready or why we aren't the right person or why this isn't the right time. We convince ourselves it's physically, mentally, and emotionally better to stay on our same old rock.

But we are out of alignment with ourselves.

Illness, weight gain, lethargy, and more are the gifts of living in our comfort zone. Sometimes we deal with this by mustering the energy to take on a change that is small, believing that this safer venture will appease our truer longing to jump out of our comfort zone to that other rock. While this may placate us for a time, eventually the discomfort and dis-ease return, often along with more feelings of frustration.

Can We Decide to Make Change Easy?

The short answer is, yes, we can decide to make change easy. We decide whether to make situations and circumstances difficult or manageable. We decide what our relationship with change is like. We decide whether or not to accept responsibility for our actions and feelings. Depending on what we choose, we determine what happens next. These decisions have significant impact on our mental, physical, and social health and well-being – personally and professionally. When we are intentional, we build muscle that helps us explore our thoughts and feelings, which leads to the gathering of important information that leads us to opportunities to do reality checks, and that leads to clarity.

Fear can keep us in our comfort zone. Fear and all of the other physical and emotional signs and symptoms inform us that we are exploring new territory. Fear is a safety mechanism that kicks in whether there is real or perceived danger. It's up to us to decide whether the warning is warranted or is a false alarm.

Staying focused on the big picture and the opportunity to make a real difference moves us from *naval gazing* – over-analyzing our situation from a *this is all about me* perspective – to a *this is about us* perspective. When we seek to make a difference, we look for opportunities and openings that benefit our staff, teams, and the business. This outward-viewing perspective also allows us to keep from staying too far *in* the day-to-day business, where we are less needed, and gets us working squarely *on* the business, where our leadership is required.

Venturing outside of our comfort zone will change our perspective and provide openings for growth. As humans, our ability to adapt and adjust is crucial to our wellness at every level. When we become too comfortable or rely on our past achievements to carry us in the present, we reduce our ability to thrive.

When we seek to build relationships and communicate our vision, we build trust, transparency, and connections that will help provide the tools and ladders we need. We don't have to conform. It actually isn't in our best interest. Rather, the best kind of change comes from seeking to define who we really are.

Aligning your values and beliefs with your vision is a powerful formula for change.

Here's the opportunity for you to be someone who makes a difference.

What Do I Really Want?

*"Passion is energy. Feel the power that
comes from focusing on what excites you."*
—Oprah Winfrey

K nowing what we really want can be a challenge.
Often when I ask clients what they really want,
their answer is something like this: "I don't want
to feel this way" or "I don't want to be stuck." But the most
common answer is, "I don't really know what I want, but

I can tell you what I don't want." People seem to readily know what they don't want, but cannot as easily say what they do want.

Whether within an organization or in our personal lives, we are reticent about openly admitting and declaring what we really want. And so we often put what we really want on the back burner, deciding it just isn't possible. And then we trudge on.

What Can Light Bulb Moments Do for Us?

I love how people light up when you allow them to share their dreams, to share what they really want. Their feelings of joy, wonder, and curiosity tumble forth, unrestrained. I call these *light bulb moments*, times when we are inspired, enlightened, and open to possibilities. These moments are what I enjoy most about my work: helping organizations and individuals become inspired and, as a result, see themselves and their circumstance differently. The world is full of promise and possibility from this place of openness.

Not owning what we want can wreak havoc on our careers and in our personal lives. When we focus on what we don't want, we actively push away what we do want. We've invited what we don't want into our psyches and, thus, into our lives. Then the thing we don't want is the thing we end up having to figure out how to get rid of – and that includes mental clutter, physical clutter, and relationship clutter.

My first mentor, Doris – our neighbor who was in her 50s when I was ten years old – taught me the value of having folks around who are willing to give advice. Over the years, she turned into a sponsor as she navigated a few opportunities for me to make money and have professional experiences. Since then, I've engaged countless mentors, advisors, counselors, and coaches. Learning how to say what I need and to say it out loud – speaking past any fears of judgment, retribution, or horror – has been one of the most helpful things for my career and my personal life. In those mentoring and advising relationships, I feel able to be honest with myself and to prioritize my needs rather than focusing on the other roles and responsibilities I have. My wellness team, as I call my advisors, is who I go to in order to figure out what I really want.

When we grow tired of our circumstances to the point of wanting to release the pain, we are ready to ask ourselves what we really want. I've sat on any number of couches and chairs, drunk tea or wine, and spoken through tears, trying to answer the same question each time I've met with a trusted advisor: "What do I really want?"

A few years ago, I found myself back in a state of frustration, which had led to a sense of confusion, and I felt a strong sense of turmoil about making a couple of big decisions, one personal and one professional. Both were about letting go of much-loved and invested-in relationships. Sitting, once again, with one of my wellness coaches, the dreaded question came at me before I had even gotten comfortable in my chair. She asked, "Why are you here? What do you want?" Without much thought, the words "I want to breathe" exhaled out of me. She came back at me with, "What does that mean?" My surprised response was, "I don't know exactly, but I guess I'm here to figure that out."

What was so clear to me was that I didn't have to think long or hard about what I wanted. I was suffocating under the weight of those relationships, figuratively and literally. Several respiratory illnesses later, I much more fully understood the meaning of my blurted statement of "I want to breathe." My body was physically presenting me with important information that supported what I already knew: I needed to breathe.

When we ignore our intuition, it manifests somewhere in our bodies. We often ignore our bodies until something tragic happens. Even then, we may still choose not to act in our own best interest.

Why do we hold ourselves to contracts or commitments we made to ourselves and others when we were at a very different place and time in our relationship life? Rather than revisit the contract to see if it is still relevant, and renegotiate if it's not, we plod on. The discomfort of having the conversation involved holds us hostage and we continue to be engaged in something that no longer serves us.

We also worry about what "people" will think. The perceived judgment of others is a heavy burden for many of us. We have reputations and status and we believe this to be most important. We see change as a weakness. We identify with stereotypes or untruths about what it is to be a leader, manager, partner, parent. If we don't live up to those expectations, if we opt out, we see that as failure. And we consider failure to be weakness. I've yet to meet anyone who says they are comfortable with failure or with being seen as weak.

All of that is ego driven. The ego rides our thoughts, feelings, and behaviors if we allow it to run unbridled. That will work, if what you really want is to please everyone else. Just be clear that it's a choice you're making. But, if you find that pleasing everyone else isn't working for you; that living up to expectations you set for yourself but that no longer align with who you really are; or that the stereotype of what it means to be x, y, or z is no longer practical – then it's time to put ego aside and get clear about what it is you really do want and who it is you want to be.

Can We Fly the Plane Before It's Been Built?

At the end of the day, we have to come clean with ourselves about what we need and trust that what is to follow that moment of knowing is on its way. We don't need all the answers or a map for how to get there right this minute or by the end of the day. We don't need a long list of to-do items. We can simply accept that we have just realized and uttered our most honest statement of what we really want, maybe without even thinking it through or without having to search long and hard. Over the next few weeks and months that follow, we will learn a great deal about what it means to want what we want and how to achieve that.

For now, just breathe into the relief of claiming your truth.

When we pay attention to what we want and how that shows up in our bodies, we learn to trust our instincts. We learn to be motivated by what matters to us rather than by conventional thinking. That internal motivation is often experienced as bursts of energy and excitement sustained over time. That's *passion*.

What would happen if we lead ourselves with the passion of aligning with our values?

Moreover, what if we trust that we can build the plane while we are flying it? In doing so, we ask ourselves to experience a level of ambiguity and keep moving forward even so. We don't know exactly what sort of plane we'll land with, but we do know we are capable of building exactly what is needed. We trust our intuition and instinct, we apply our skills, experience, and knowledge, and we ask for and get the right support and expertise as we need it. Because we are open to more possibilities, we realize that there are many right ways, many paths to success, and many answers to the questions we have as we create what we really want.

Getting stuck in the belief that there is only one way to arrive at a destination stifles the opportunity to entertain new ideas and methods along the way. We don't adapt and recalibrate, but keep trying to fly the same exact flight pattern. That struggle takes an enormous amount of effort and drains us of energy and resources. We can toil and labor and never take off, or we can calmly and intentionally use our energy and resources efficiently to create synergy and lift-off.

Can You Shift Your Experience?

Remember what it feels like when things come together and line up when we had thought it wouldn't happen? Remember the excitement that builds as we get closer to identifying solutions? It's that heart-racing, energy-buzzing that makes us feel alive and very grateful to be in that very moment. Notice that those feelings and experiences aren't so different from the ones we encounter when fear crops up. The difference is our perception. Our perspective about one experience is excitement and engagement and our perspective about the other is dread and disconnection.

What we really want is to feel alive, useful, connected with purpose and intention, engaged in our work and with our staff and teams, our family and partner. When we are clear about what that looks, sounds, and feels like, we can evaluate opportunities for growth based on criteria we know to be our place of synergy. The information is right there, in our bodies, and we can choose to tap into it.

When we choose to perceive change as opportunity rather than threat, we can more easily know what we want, and what we want becomes crystal clear. When we don't over-analyze and over-think it; we know without having to muster much effort what it is we want. When we pay attention to our bodies, which provide very specific information regarding our alignment with our truth, we continue to grow forward, and we more easily move through fear and into passion.

When we accept that there are many pathways that can lead us to discover the outcomes we desire, we accept ambiguity as a partner in building the right plane for our right flight.

How Do I Get
What I Really Want?

*"Go confidently in the direction of your dreams!
Live the life you always imagined. As you simplify
your life, the laws of the universe will be simpler."*
—**Henry David Thoreau**

H ow we get what we really want isn't so different
from how we get what we don't want. It's all
about what we focus on. If what we really want

61

is to be of use, to have purpose, and to be connected to others, then our focus and actions ought to align with those things – and our experience of them will follow.

We may think that getting what we want means others don't get what they want, but when we think in those binary terms, our outcomes will follow suit.

A close friend and colleague and I once had a very long conversation about several topics that all had to do with his perception that in business some win and so others lose. "That's the way things roll," he said. He shared with me that as he approached negotiations with unions, contractors or new hires, he was out to win. He felt that getting what he wanted meant that the other folks might get frustrated, unhappy, or be unaware that they weren't getting the best end of the deal, but that he would ultimately get what he wanted – which was good for his business. He took it in stride that he was going to be the bad guy in their minds, and his solace was that he felt he was doing the right thing.

When I asked him how he felt when that happened to him, when the roles were reversed, he shrugged it off and said that he could accept that it was how the game was played. "Sometimes I win. Sometimes I don't." But the change in his energy and posture as he uttered those words was significant. He'd gone from confident, eager, and engaged to quiet and still, and his voice had taken on a passive tone. I pointed out the stark contrast in his body language and his tone and he laughed. He laughed even louder when I suggested that perhaps he should consider how win-win situations might be a better way to lead.

Getting what we really want is inextricably linked to helping others get what they want.

Leaders who are able to create win–win situations are highly effective and influential – and they get what they want. We all want to feel that we are being given the best opportunity, and that we are offering the best opportunity. Doing so requires transparency and vulnerability. The way we feel about ourselves and the way others feel about themselves as we engage in problem-solving, negotiation, and day-to-day transactions sets the stage for the type of relationships we have – and the opportunities that follow.

Bringing our best allows others to bring their best.

Who Do You Think You Are?

Maybe we grew up in a time and place when wanting more than what we had seemed greedy, selfish, and perhaps even too ambitious for our own good. Those of us who are part of the boomer generation were raised to assume that jobs were scarce, so if we got one we should hold onto it for dear life. If we were lucky enough to have a house, car, and vacation, we should be grateful and not push our luck. In secret, we held our wishes and dreams close to our vests, kept them hidden deep inside ourselves for fear of discovery. Many of us let those dreams and desires go, in favor of more pressing roles or responsibilities.

We carry that experience into our workplaces and spaces. We may wish for the corner office, the plumb assignment, the opportunity to work abroad, or to lead a major change initiative, but we wish secretly. We hold that desire close to the vest, telling no one or barely uttering the words aloud because, "Who are we to want more than we have?"

This quote from Marianne Williamson's writing has made a deep impact on me: "Our deepest fear is not that we are inadequate. Our deepest fear is that we are powerful beyond measure. It is our light, not our darkness, that most frightens us. Our playing small does not serve the world. There is nothing enlightened about shrinking so that other people won't feel insecure around you." I discovered it at a time when I was really trying to figure who I thought I was to believe I could make a difference.

As I read those words, I was nearly dumbfounded by how off-center my thinking had been, how self-absorbed and responsibility-relinquishing. Why would I abandon myself and resign myself to less than my own potential? Williamson's words helped me realize that there was every reason I should speak my wishes and desires aloud – every reason to feel engaged and deeply connected to my work and my life. Because, as I liberated myself, I gave others permission to do the same.

What Would You Do If You Could Not Fail?

Often when speaking at conferences or providing leadership training, I ask the crowd this question: "If you could do anything you wanted, without worry about money or failure, what would you do?" I watch folks contemplate the question and I see smiles cross their faces, heads nod or shake back and forth with acknowledgement, and hands go up because people want to share their yearnings.

Feeling that we have permission to dream and believe is such an exciting and enjoyable experience. Everything about us changes instantaneously. We flush with excitement, our hearts race, and our imaginations soar with aspiration. We are free, if only momentarily, from the guilt and anguish we experience when we only covet what we really want without reaching for it.

Then when I ask the group, "What can we do to make what you want happen?" the tone and energy shifts dramatically and the excuses fly.

It's when we have the audacity to believe we can have whatever we dream that those dreams become possible. As we shift our thoughts from *can't* to *can* and *won't* to *will*, we shift our paradigm and open ourselves to possibility.

Will You Ask for What You Want?

Remember the old adage to be careful what you ask for? It's usually said as a dire warning to someone who has uttered something they really wish for. We chuckle at the admonition and try to brush it off, but also bristle a bit at the warning. The reality is that the saying is true: What we ask for is what we usually get, because that's where our focus is.

Rather than cower in uncertainty and fear, we can embrace what we really want, get clear and specific about that, and then ask for it and focus on it. If it's true that we get what we ask for, then let's ask for what we *really* want, and leave what we don't want as a passing, impractical thought that does not require our energy or attention.

Articulate what you really want. Write it down with all of the specificity that provides clarity. What does what you want look like, sound like, and feel like? What will you be doing, saying, and thinking differently when you have it? What will others do and say differently then? What are your intended outcomes? What are some of the potential unintended outcomes?

Saying out loud what we really want and engaging with the physiological and emotional energy associated with it, we become familiar with and can interpret information as it comes in, which brings us ever closer to what we want.

Tell others what you really want. We sometimes hold our ideas back out of fear that, once shared or spoken aloud, others will steal them from us. The notion that withholding our ideas will keep them ours alone is unproductive. More than once, I've held onto an idea or thought with that same thinking and then someone else who had the same idea moved forward with it. Every time I've experienced that I was disappointed that I hadn't gone ahead with the idea and realized I'd let it sit too long.

Elizabeth Gilbert writes about this concept in her book *Big Magic*. I couldn't help but nod my head in agreement and laugh out loud with a bit of acknowledging naiveté as she shared the story of how she had a great book idea that she didn't follow through with and how another author, Ann Patchett, wrote that same book, though they had never discussed the idea. I honestly thought I had imagined it when similar things had happened to me. Even worse, sometimes I'd chastise myself for thinking I was so clever to have been the only one to have had a particular idea. Of course others are having great ideas all of the time. The difference is that some of us are willing to step out and make those ideas into reality and others are only willing to sit back waiting for the perfect moment to take action.

There is no perfect moment. There is only now.

When we share what we want with others, we open ourselves to finding support systems, mentors, connections, and resources to turn what we want into reality. Others become willing participants in supporting us to get what we want. Simply put, others cannot help us get what we really want if they have no idea what that is. Holding back is a stalling tactic and a statement that we are not ready or willing to move forward.

Great ideas will come forth one way or the other. If you aren't willing to follow through, let the idea go. The next one will be along shortly.

Sometimes we are the support or catalyst for bringing forth an idea, but are not the intended carrier to bring it to life. It may be our role to germinate an idea and then allow the opportunity and possibility for someone else to take that seed, tend to it as the roots grow, until it blooms and flourishes.

If, however, you know that you want to make a difference at work and you know it's what you really want because it makes you light up and smile, makes you feel something emotionally and physically that you recognize as excitement and passion – then claim out loud your intention to make it happen. Share it with your colleagues, staff, and team so you and they can experience how it unfolds.

Are You Too Attached?

At times, we become so passionate or certain about what we want that we get very prescriptive about the details. We get too attached about specifics and think we know exactly how things should and will unfold. When we get too attached to specific details we can get in our own way of making what we really want happen because we cannot see or hear what is in front of us. We may become inflexible and headstrong. Forcing what we really want to materialize is akin to forcing others to do what we want. It doesn't work and it builds frustration, dissatisfaction, and defeat.

When we are too attached, when we insist on getting things done in a very specific way, when we take credit for opportunities and successes and ignore those who helped us along the way, we are forgetting to offer trust and gratitude to the process. We hinder opportunities from coming our way because we can't see them for the gifts they really are.

When we allow what we want to materialize, it's our acknowledgement and appreciation that keeps the flow of energy and opportunity fluid. We don't need to apologize for receiving what we want, nor do we downplay our role in being clear and open and willing. Saying things like, "I'm just lucky, I guess" or "It fell into my lap" undermines our involvement and our greater purpose and promise.

Being grateful for and acknowledging those who have brought opportunities to us, by thanking them, will bring more opportunities. Honesty, humility, and gratitude will help others continue to bring what is needed and keeps us in the stance of being an open vessel for receiving continued abundance.

Is There Enough?

Managers, leaders, and social entrepreneurs often worry that there is not enough money or resources to support their endeavors. When we are caught up in thinking there isn't enough – not enough money, resources, people, or time – we set the tone for shortages to come our way. Rather than expressing gratitude for what *has* come, we see our coffers as half-empty. We fill ourselves, our team, and our supporters at all levels with the sense that there is not enough and there may not be more coming. We shrug our shoulders and say, "Well, we tried."

There is more than enough. There is more than enough money, resources, people, and time. Don't agree? Check out the Apple Store when the latest iPhone launch is happening. Drive through the Whole Foods parking lot on a Saturday morning. Examine closely the funding provided to a new project at a company. Watch how the social entrepreneur raises the funds to test and launch a new product. The resources are available. The resources we need and will need will be there.

Use gratitude for what you already have to shift your belief. Believe that the resources exist and allow yourself to believe they will be brought to you as you need them.

Isn't Giving Better Than Receiving?

Learning to receive is a critical piece of getting what you really want. This is something I've had to train myself to do. Raised to be fiercely independent and to work hard for what I want, as well as to expect nothing to come to me without working really hard for it, made receiving difficult. I interpreted being given to as a sign or a judgment that I was irresponsible, lazy, and not capable.

It is difficult to accept what we think we do not deserve or we believe we have not earned. Locked in this vicious cycle, we can drive away what we really want without knowing we are doing so. Expecting to get what we want means being open to receiving it, and allowing the possibility that it may come in very unexpected and unusual ways, from all sorts of individuals and entities.

When we accept that we are worthy of receiving, we step into a world of promise and possibility. Coming from a place of strength and confidence supports our use of the gifts we receive through all manner of thoughtful, intentional, and gracious channels.

As we name what we want, claim it, accept that there are the resources we need, are ready to receive, we must also take action. Many of my clients and colleagues stop short of taking action. We must be willing to move in the direction of what we really want. Moving from ideation to creation is critical.

We create when we act as though what we really want is possible and is about to become our reality. This can be as simple as dressing for the promotion we want, engaging our focused attention in planning meetings, or enrolling in trainings, classes, or certification programs. Action is required to get what we really want.

All of this may sound kind of "woo woo," as though little effort is required from us beyond marshaling out thoughts, but the reality is that getting what we really want is a practical process that requires active participation from us – mentally and physically. The connections between our perceptions, thoughts, and actions support the steps of naming what we want, claiming it as ours, opening ourselves to receiving, and dealing with gremlins that say we don't deserve what we want. This takes resolute intention, concerted determination, and perseverance.

Here's what's on the other side of getting practical and actively participating in going after what we want: opportunity, possibility, positivity, and the probability of success. And it is there, in that space, that we find purpose, meaning, and connection. This is where we define success on our own terms and, thus, measure our success in ways that are aligned with who we really are, rather than who we are pretending to be or who people expect us to be. This is where we find great purpose and meaning in life. It happens when our focus begins inward then turns outward.

When we change ourselves, we are then able to see our ideas as great opportunities for others, and we become motivated by newfound purpose.

Chapter 6

What Happens If I Need to Change Again?

"Be deliberate and afraid of nothing."
—Audre Lorde

Once we've navigated the unchartered waters of change, we naturally lean into the new normal we've set for ourselves. The shift in our perceptions and thoughts from *can't* to *can* and *won't* to *will*, the modification of our emotions from fear to promise, and the ease of our actions toward the direction of what we really want become part of our new normal. We move forward with confidence and assurance, motivated and energized as we provide opportunities to the people we lead and manage and to our organizations.

Frequently repeated thoughts or behaviors become new habits. Like defense mechanisms, habits can be extremely useful – until they no longer work. Living on automatic is what many of us do. There are times, however – like when we are confronted with new situations, circumstances, and people – when we can find ourselves struggling to maintain our new habits. Left unchecked and without our conscious intention, our well-formed habits can slowly erode. Or our new habits can become ingrained, persisting even when it's time to change again.

A sort of uneasy feeling in the pit of our stomach grows as each day passes. We may have the idea that "We've been here before," but just as that thought crosses our minds we quickly cast it aside.

We experience setbacks in our ability to proactively advance ourselves and our ideas. We lose sight and miss the fork in the road and turn back, troubled by the prospect of yet another change. We experience confusion and loss along the way as those we have given our trust and loyalty to – those we believed to be allies, friends, colleagues – deeply challenge us.

When this happens, it's time to turn the focus inward again and do the work to get clear about what we really want.

What Happens When Others Get Stuck?

As participants on boards and senior leadership teams, or while engaging in leadership as a staff member, volunteer, or consultant, we've likely experienced some hair-raising moments. There is often a point in a meeting where we suddenly have a feeling of dread that we've been here before. It's a moment of clarity that the issue being discussed is not a new one and the solutions being discussed are also not new. The wagons may have been circling around this issue for quite some time. The team is stuck and so are the individuals around the table.

I worked with a senior-level executive who was trying to lead a major change effort, and she had this very experience. She realized in the middle of an important meeting that she had been there before, with that same group, having that same conversation. As we discussed her moment of clarity, she said with shock, "I've been here with this group before. In fact, several times before." What shocked her the most was her realization that she was just as stuck as the team was. She hadn't seen that aspect before. As someone who identified herself as a change leader and fostered her own professional growth and development, she was stunned. She wondered aloud how she had gotten there. Over several months, we unraveled what had lead her back into old patterns and behaviors in that situation, and she was able to see a way to change the stuck pattern.

When we are motoring through work and life on automatic pilot, we sometimes forget that we need to have an emergency road kit. We don't make time for and so don't keep up the daily maintenance needed in order to keep our lives running at our best performance level. As such, when we encounter a bump in the road we may find ourselves unprepared to deal with the circumstances. So, to get over this bump, we find a makeshift way out and we come up with an explanation that can become a perpetual stop-gap measure. We fail to deal with the *core* problem and, almost unknowingly, focus on the symptoms.

If we don't take the time and space necessary to ensure that we are paying attention to our intentions, staying connect to what we really want, then, eventually, the wheels will fall off and we will find ourselves – just as my client did – stunned at the outcome.

Who's on Your Team?

How do we maintain ourselves for high performance in the world of work? We foster consistent practices that support our personal and professional well-being. Self-care is a critical piece of how we build resilience at work and beyond.

What do you do for self-care? Who is on your well-being team? Do you have a self-care team?

In order to build resilience at work, you need your own AAA team. No race car driver is on the track without a crew ready to support them. No professional athlete trains without a coach and a well-articulated fitness plan. Singers, writers, and CEOs have teams of people who help them train, plan, and implement success strategies. Such teams provide built-in resilience support for when times get tough, for when we don't feel like performing, are tired, or are no longer sure why we are out there doing what we do. These are the folks who help keep us on course and help us constantly improve.

Yet, we finish degrees, obtain certificates, and attend professional development seminars, then walk away as though we are no longer in need of support, feedback, or thought partners. But we do a huge disservice to ourselves and to those we work with, lead, and manage when we short-change ourselves on getting the support we need.

Developing relationships at the office, within our profession, or with folks who hold our ideal job can help us. We can connect, share our thoughts and ideas, and get necessary insight and feedback. Mentors, sponsors, and coaches can play important roles on our support team. When things get tough or we feel puzzled, the trusted members of our support team are there for us to lean on and learn from.

Effort or Efficiency?

Somehow we've confused *work* with *getting things done*. We increase the number of hours, projects, and activities beyond that which can be reasonably completed, and extend our workdays in an effort to manage the increasing expectations. We pretend that we are efficient and effective and try to become more dedicated employees and leaders.

What suffers as a result? Our health and wellness, and our relationships outside of work.

Like any athlete, racecar driver, or performer, we are most efficient when we put in the number of hours and the level of energy that allows us to get results while also staying healthy and prepared for the big moments. Lack of sleep, lack of exercise, poor nutrition – eventually they will all lead beyond dis-ease to disease. But we seem to wear dark circles under our eyes and carry gigantic cups of coffee all day long as badges of honor – "Hey, I'm part of the loyalty club." In reality, they are badges showing that we lack healthy boundaries for ourselves.

When we abandon ourselves through lack of self-care and consideration for our own well-being, we become the accident waiting to happen. Eventually, something comes along and we snap.

We set the tone and the pace of our work. Through our example, we also set expectations around boundaries for our team. We may evaluate the performance of our team through our skewed lens if we are not maintaining self-care. We may then think the problem is that our team isn't as loyal or as hard-working as we are, despite their great performance, and so we pass over people rather than learning from them.

How Do We Know When We Are Successful?

How *we* measure our own success is what matters. Yet, so often, we allow others to define what our success looks like, from deciding on the number of years it took you to make partner to our titles, paychecks and on and on. External motivators are not inherently bad, they just don't serve us well if they aren't how *we* define our success.

As we set our goals and objectives, we also need to take the time to articulate what benchmarks will demonstrate that we are moving forward. What we measure matters.

When we learn to disrupt patterns and habits that no longer serve us, and replace them with the tools and methods I've shared here, we offer ourselves opportunities to solve problems and make decisions that support our well-being and that of our teams. If we allow ourselves to be life-long learners, then every experience is transformed into a process designed to give us important information. We slowly eliminate all of the drama and learn to be realistic and optimistic.

Going the leadership path alone is a huge gamble. When we lead, we collaborate and we build relationships, and this requires solid support systems. These are the critical elements of our ability to manage and support change for ourselves and our organizations. The challenge is to silent the ego to give voice to the change agent that is present in all of us, dare we to listen.

We can opt to begin anew each time a change opportunity arises. When we get clear about what we really want, we can be intentional about the direction we want to go. We can learn from the experiences we've had and apply their lessons to our current circumstances. We can remain open to possibilities and opportunities. The choice is ours. And the choice we make is the difference that will make the difference – either way.

How Does My Life Look Now?

"The heaviness of being successful was replaced by the lightness of being a beginner again, less sure about everything. It freed me to enter one of the most creative periods of my life"
—Steve Jobs

Seldom do we look back and say, "I wish I hadn't changed." More often, we are grateful to and for the experiences and opportunities that create the change we seek. When we're grateful, we open up to making a difference for those who are asked to follow our lead. We can navigate and move beyond the, at times, transactional nature of leadership and professional relationships and understand more about how our perceptions, thoughts, and behaviors, when they are in alignment with our values, propel us forward.

Clearly, our willingness to engage in personal change is essential to our ability to lead change. When we are willing, we no longer wait for others or for circumstances to change. We are no longer the backseat driver in our careers; we take the wheel and determine our own direction.

The example we set is the key. As we unlock our own satisfaction, we unlock and open doors for those we lead.

What Does Work Feel Like Now?

When we are in a place of *alignment*, our values, thoughts, and perceptions lead our actions and responses. We are powerful and capable beyond measure. Synergy occurs and propels our intentions into action. Highly productive, we are poised and able to make opportunities materialize, resources become available, collaborations occur. We create what we are trying to create, what our companies need.

Our overall feeling of well-being becomes infectious. As we engage our support teams, as we hold to our personal wellness plan, we sustain momentum so that we are buoyed in good times and in times of struggle. We give ourselves permission to lead and to do so in ways that support the ebb and flow of work and life. In doing so, we build teams, departments, and companies that enjoy constructive, productive, and effective work spaces. We encourage and support the personal and professional growth of those who report to and work with us. The collaboration and cooperation of people working in such environments improves job satisfaction, employee retention, and loyalty.

As we look internally to ourselves to define what our success looks like, we free ourselves from worry and concern about what others think, thus also decreasing our interest in judging others against erroneous measures of success. We are far more compassionate.

When we are able to express empathy for ourselves, we can extend it to others. We drop the pretense and get to the heart of human connection.

At the end of the day, most of us want to feel like we have been of some use; like we have been seen, heard, and appreciated for our presence and contributions. We can deliver this gift to ourselves and to our staff and teams. We have the opportunity to lead from a place of engagement and responsiveness. When we step into our potential, we afford others the same opening.

When our work and our leadership presence are filled with a sense of calm and clarity, our leadership is natural and straightforward. We deal with difficult people, problems, and projects with grace and confidence.

We create a space where magic happens.

Why is that?

It's because having a sense of wonder, anticipation, connection, centeredness, can-do, and will-do opens unlimited possibilities. We pass all of that along to the people we lead. Then our teams are at their best for solving problems, innovating, and creating new opportunities.

This place of standing in our own personal power is where we are most vulnerable – and yet it is also where we are most powerful, because whenever we are genuine we are empowered. When we lead aligned with who we really are, we establish ourselves as reliable, dependable, accessible, and approachable.

Are You Ready to Lead?

This is a point of reckoning. As we step into our potential and expand our influence and ability we ready ourselves for the limelight that comes along with our success. Fear of success and what it may bring can keep us accepting mediocrity. But the safety we tell ourselves we feel by lurking behind the scenes, by not stepping into our own limelight, by doing enough but not too much, by showing only a little of our ability so that we keep our positions, by not asking for what we really want – that is all an illusion that we hide behind to support a state of limitation.

When we lead from personal authenticity, what shines through is not pretentious ego but the powerful and limitless beings we really are. And we gain the ability to show others how to shine as themselves, too.

Each day is a clean slate. We show up and begin again with fresh intention and focus and with the tools in hand to make happen what we really want to happen each day.

Today, right now, is the perfect time to shine.

Acknowledgements

There are so many people to thank for their contributions to my leadership experiences and, thus, for the inspiration and experiential education that helped formulate my ideas and provided the bones for this book. From mentors and sponsors, researchers and writers, fellowship and leadership cohorts, and women executive cohorts, to mentees, clients, and accomplices – many of the contributors are trusted colleagues, advisors, and friends. Just as many are acquaintances who, through their examples, their sharing of ideas, and their proficiencies, gave me such generous support, even though they may not have had known I was one of the many they were supporting.

This book would not have come to life without the fabulous Angela Lauria. Grace Kerina, an editing wizard, helped refine my ideas and thoughts toward coherent passages, paragraphs, and chapters. I thank them both for their thoughtful and dedicated partnership. Thanks to Danielle Miller for the "percolate" that created the book's subtitle. Grateful to Martha Pearson Langer, Pear Ink Design, for her web technology and design support. Thanks to my publisher Morgan James Publishing for your behind the scenes dedication to my book.

My thanks to my colleagues, friends, and family, for their unceasing support and for nudging me to write. A special thanks goes out to my dear friends Robin, Nuria, Olivia, and Jeanne for encouraging me to put my voice into the arena.

To those of you I haven't yet met and those of you I may never meet, who read this book, thank you for choosing to read these pages and for the honor and privilege of being a part of your journey.

And, finally, thank you JMR—so grateful for your love and support.

About the Author

Marcia Coné is a writer, speaker, change strategist, and advocate for women. As founding CEO of the Women's Fund of Rhode Island, she successfully advocated for policy advances, including women's leadership, representation, and paid family leave. Her activism continues through her writing, speaking, and consulting with philanthropic, corporate, and government organizations. The author lives in East Greenwich, Rhode Island and Vienna, Austria.

marcia-cone.com
https://www.facebook.com/marciaconeconsulting/
twitter.com/mac_ri
www.linkedin.com/in/marcia-coné

Thank You

For a short video demonstration of Marcia's power of engagement, visit www.marcia-cone.com/video.

Thank you for reading and for doing the challenging but rewarding work of getting clear and stepping up. Leaders who are clear about what they want and know how to get what they want are more productive, innovative, and satisfied. My hope is that you are that kind of leader.

I wish you the very best on your leadership journey.

Morgan James makes all of our titles available
through the Library for All Charity Organizations.

www.LibraryForAll.org